ROB MARTIN

First published in 2021

This book is copyright under the Berne Convention. All rights are reserved. Apart from any fair dealing for the purpose of private study, research, criticism or review, as permitted under the Copyright Act, 1956, no part of this publication may be reproduced, stored in a retrieval system, or transmitted, in any form or by any means, electronic, electrical, chemical, mechanical, optical, photocopying, recording or otherwise, without the prior permission of the copyright owner. Enquiries should be sent to the publishers at the undermentioned address:

EMPIRE PUBLICATIONS
1 Newton Street, Manchester M1 1HW
© Rob Martin 2021

ISBN: 978-1-909360-88-4

FOREWORD

The frenzy of an international crisis; the mammalian impulse to hoard; the foibles of local yokels, it's all here, observed and archived by England's artist answer to Switzerland's army knife: Painter, muralist, underground comic artist, television animator, cartoonist, and humorist, Rob Martin. Martin's signature style captures the flavor of his environs with wit and sensitivity. His sharp eye for character crystalizes types out of incidents; relateable, appealing, uproarious. Treat yourself and a friend to his tart humor, and find yourself chuckling through the day as you see the icons in Martin's book playing out in the humans around you.

Sue Bielenberg

Animation Artist on *The Simpsons*, *King of the Hill*, *Rugrats*, *Dilbert*, *Dragon Tales*, *The Oblongs*, *Mr. Sprinkles*, *Harmonquest*.

INTRODUCTION

In 2020 my 90 year-old father had his shopping trolley pulled from him by a woman in her 50's. Her tirade of abuse and the act of grabbing my dad's shopping trolley as panic buyers pulled food and toilet rolls from the shelves, stripping bare the supermarket, was typical of the panic as the Covid pandemic began.

In November 2019 I had been involved in a serious car accident and had still not fully recovered by the time Covid hit the UK. It was through 2020 that these illustrations were drawn. Trying to make sense of the pandemic by sending it up. A little bit of truth is in all the work. I guess art can flow through times of uncertainty. These cartoons are fuelled by strange observations of entitled, selfish people. None I could see had ever put their head down on a motorway having been in a collision.

Rob Martin

ACKNOWLEDGEMENTS

Thanks to: Joanne Whitaker (scanning pages), Drew Hartley (technical help), Dave Savage (cover lettering), Stuart Hoyle and staff at 'Calder Graphics' (art supplies), Milnsbridge News (being open throughout 2020).

DEDICATION

This book is dedicated to Nino Gensale. Nino was a cleaner for the NHS, this is dedicated to the laughter and friendship of 31 years.

A pensioner has a shopping cart swiped from him by an angry entitled 62 year old white woman.

A pensioner shields a pregnant woman as panic buyers swipe every last loaf of bread from the supermarket shelves.

"Yeah.. I'm working from home!"

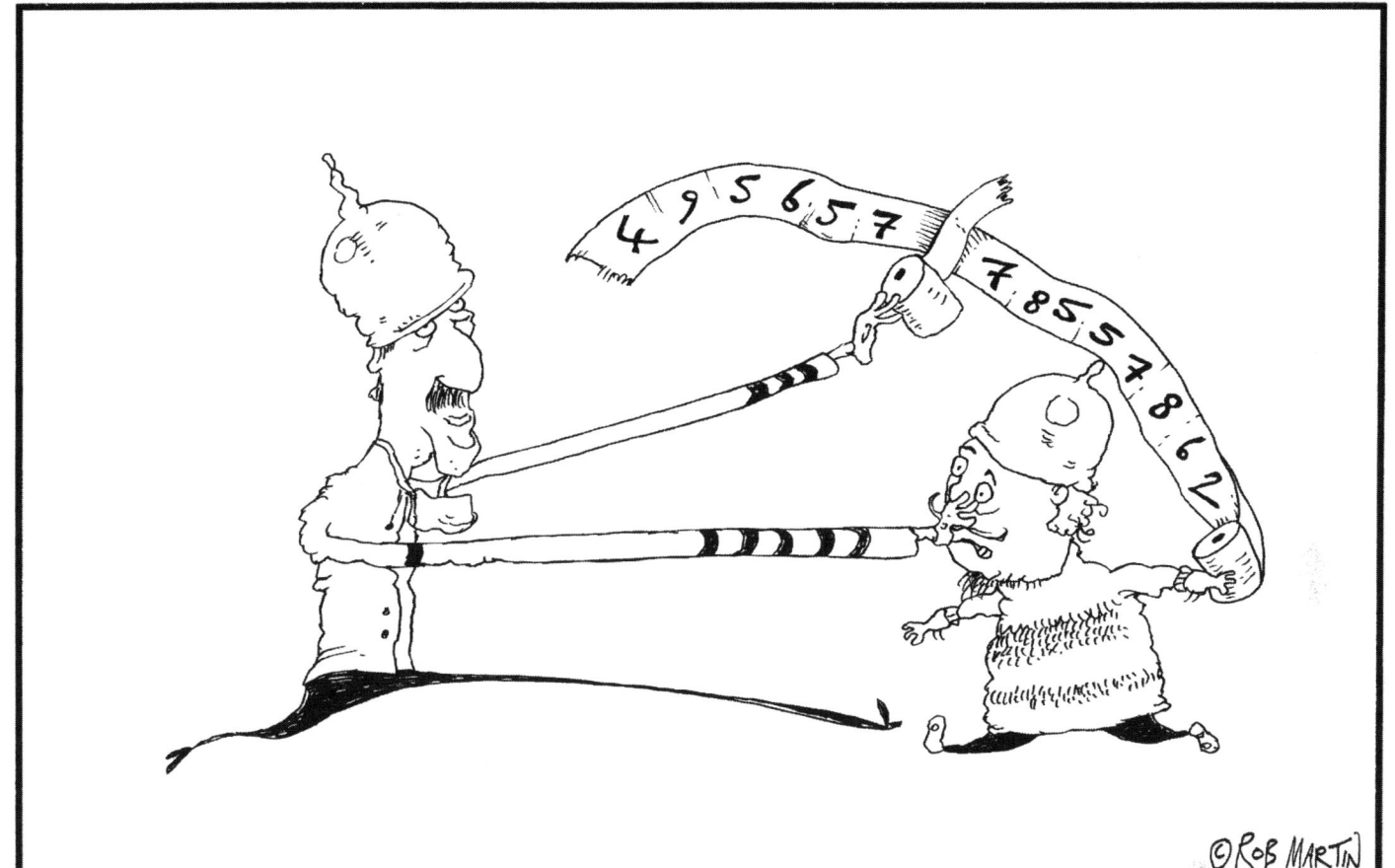

Every day for two weeks, the neighbour jet washes his porch for five hours.

Meanwhile, the other neighbour points his air rifle at a Butterfly he suspects has a virus.

Patrick starts singing 'Jolene' by Dolly Parton.

"Sorry, but... If you didn't use the hand sanitizer... You can put that back! We won't sell you it! Pump sodium laureth sulfate, hexyl cinnamel, cocamidepropyl betaine and bezophenone 4 on your hands now or leave!!!"

"I'm on this path. I'm not stopping or slowing down. You can walk faster if you have a problem!"

"Hey you.. You tramp! Let that Bird free!"

Town drunks do not understand 'social' and 'distance' are two words which go together like 'decorative' and 'concrete'.

A flotilla of joggers believe running can stop a virus.
Whilst Jeff runs after the bottle.

8p.m. every Thursday.
The public clap and play music for the health service front line workers.
Mrs. Hyde decides to perform an exorcism.

Staring at his phone, reading about social distancing.
Albert Fuzzpacket walks into Jack Bristlethwaite.

Harold the Cat is sent packing after Mr. and Mrs. Dullbrain spot him coughing on the toilet roll.

On the 2nd month of lockdown
Sir Tom Jones is seen as the only hope.

"Grrrrrrrrrrr!!!" Grunts Granville as he drops custard creams in a menacing way.

A Pharmacist leaves work feeling fabulously cosmic and groovy.
Humming 'Rockin' in the free World'.

On the second month of lockdown,
unsure if she's started hallucinating. Mrs. Scroggins asks Napoleon Frog
if he'd like another corned beef sandwich.

The conspiracy theory cult of 'The House of Sweaty Betty' pull down telecom towers with hundreds of rolls of toilet roll.

"Are you allright?!"

"Sorry! But, you can't wear gloves in here!"

The Bellend twins believe that pulling their T-shirts over their heads will protect them from viruses, rain and dub step music.

Is it a Bird? Is it a plane?
No! It's a comic shop owner
having delusional thoughts that he is 'BAT SANDWICH MAN'.

Napoleon Frog is caught looking through Mrs. Scroggins's stocking drawers. Unaware on this second month of lockdown, Mrs. Scroggins tries to figure out if hallucinations cross dress?

"Come to the punky reggae party."

At the first playground break. Tarquin the social distancing bully starts twig project fear by repeating the words. "Yoyo strepitoso!!" 24 times.

Fifteen years after the marriage.

Dave the Hamster cheers up from his pouching depression to view the daily chaotic trapped human soap opera.

It was love at first sight as Reginald couldn't smell Hilda's cheesey chips.

"I've got Cordidly!!!!"

A Bird spotter having spent too long in lockdown isn't sure, if he just heard the Wood Pigeon say, "Go eat your toilet paper and put some cream on it!"

Free delivery of chlorinated injected processed 15% Chicken pieces for only $12.95 from 'Chicken Deliver!'

"Got an order here for two bottles of sweet dry wine. Is this number 72?"

"Masks don't work! Or are you hiding something? Wait till I see you with my husband. He'll punch your lights out!"

There is nothing more terrifying than a hipster crunching down on a freshly washed apple.

The riddle of the illuminated ever lasting toilet roll.

"I must have vitamin D tablets. What do you mean sold out? I'm buying for Mrs. Iris Hum. She's got long Cordidly!!"

"Anyone got a hanky?"

Mrs. Scroggins not happy with Napoleon Frog spending his last three months staring at the ceiling wallpaper. Demands him to clean up the house.

Some people are miserable, smell of piss and curse alot.

"Why are you walking twelve feet away from me? You're mental!!"

Man with combover and no eyebrows
mocks couple wearing masks and rubber gloves.

The day the pine-apple traders statue toppled.

"Stop!! In the name of love!"

"It's all your outlook!"

"Can you lend me a tenner till Monday?"

An arrogant bus driver on the 6th week of lockdown.
Having no passengers, starts arguing with himself.
"Why is this bus late again? You stupid Zebedee ass biscuit!!"

A wild Dog chewing on a tampon is more frightening than you realise.

"Don't worry I can cover my mouth!"

The family of Sasquatches spot another abominable mask wearing thing. Will anyone believe them?

On the third month of lockdown.
Napoleon Frog brings his friend
Poodlehead Einstien for tea.

"Get your trolley out of my arse!"

A grooving cosmic starman contacts the mother ship.

"Ar Woke up this morning with the mo-fo pandemic blues!!"

Mother and son wait for a train.

Just another day shopping for Mr. Spectrumpoo.

Having spent all his furlough money on losing scratch cards, Geoffrey decides to hurl abuse at them.

Damien goes to the park.

"WTF!" Thinks Gerald.

Alternative nasal rinse Man fires off his blocked sinus.

The calamities suffered by Alan as the Fates rain toilet paper down.

"Keep going Chief!"

"Don't worry! I'm not diseased!"

"I am joyous you are going shopping
wearing the grand creation mask of sky and lightning Baba Pooji.
Here is a shiny dollar for the shopping cart!"

Jeff worries his moustache is a little overgrown.

Traditional family holiday of the summer of 2020.

"Is your tongue, two metres long?"

Mrs. Scroggins is not amused, when on month seven of a second lockdown: Napoleon Frog and Poodlehead Einstein introduce her to Freddy the butt flashing Gnome.

The angry mob disperses
after half cousin Hedley turns up
with his pet Tortoise, Suzy Creamcheese.

When jobsworth supermarket security guards become stalkers thinking Fish fingers have gone adrift.

"You know, this vaccine... It has Viagra in it.
They aren't telling anyone. You won't recognise anyone after it.
It turns you into a robot!"

Mrs. Spittle focuses on her alchemist cook book.
Creating a vaccine from Toad piss, tea tree oil, vitamin D
and a fingernail from Shakespeare.

Two nine year old boys threaten a forty year old man with a photo of a billionaire.

On the eight month, none mask wearers are put in the stocks by a mob of mask wearers and pelted with used face coverings.

"You will NOT cough on my shopping!
You will NOT cough on my shopping!
You will NOT cough on my shopping!"

"HOW ?"

Much fun was had at the social distancing formal buffet party. "I'm with my 85 year old Mother." Indicates Pandora.

"Are you neat and tidy?" Asks the manditory vaccine administer as he continues following orders.

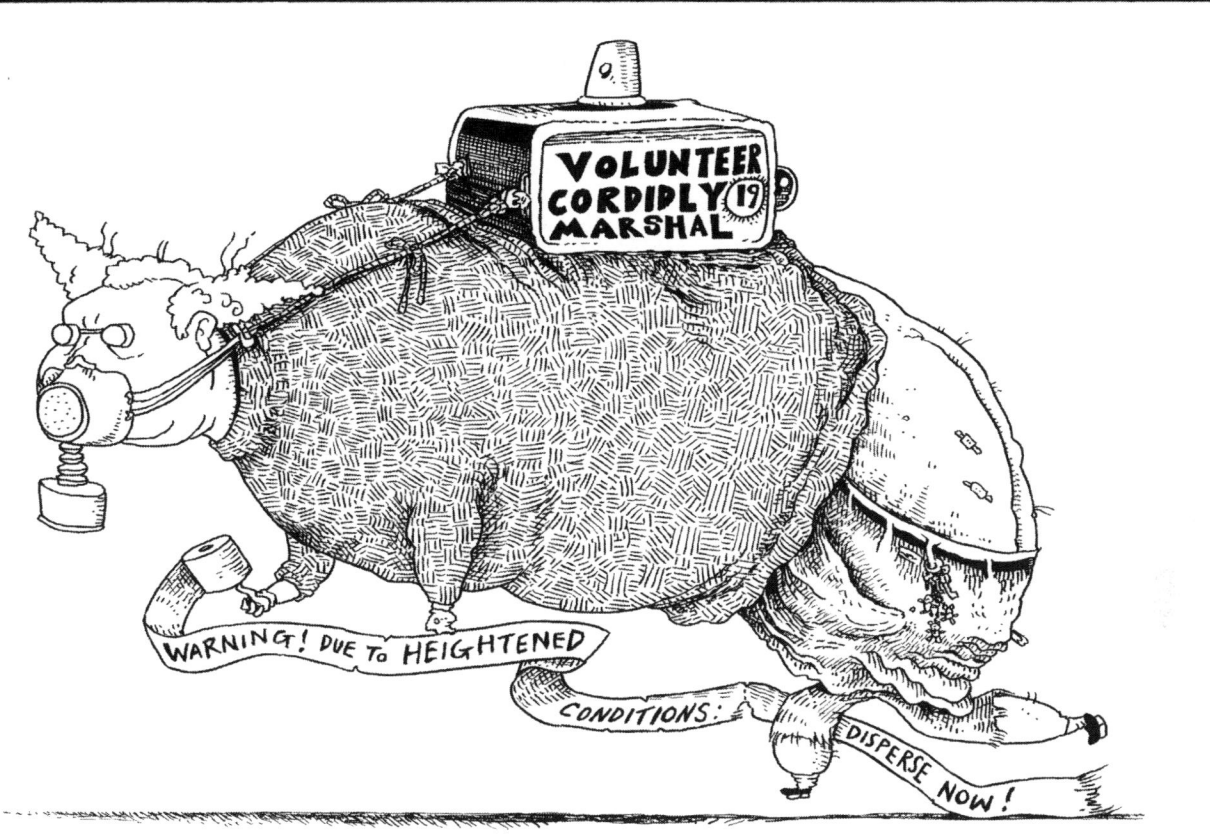

"Hey.. Those are my underpants!"

Confused by all the contradicting guidelines, Margaret has a meltdown. "Foooooooooooooooooo!!" She shouts.